The Gift

The
gift of
God is
eternal
life...

The Gift

Gordon & Gladis DePree

ZONDERVAN
PUBLISHING HOUSE
OF THE ZONDERVAN CORPORATION
GRAND RAPIDS, MICHIGAN 49506

The Gift

Second printing   1977
ISBN 0 - 310 - 23650 - 9

Library of Congress Cataloging in Publication Data

DePree, Gladis, 1933-
  The gift.

  1. Christian poetry, American.   I. DePree,
Gordon, joint author.   II. Title.
PS3554.E63G5   811'.5'4   76-4826

... the gift of God is eternal life. ...
— Romans 6:23

I look around
In a world of gifted people
And wonder, a bit wistfully,
What is my gift?
What do I have to give the world?

> *The gift of God to each of us*
> *Is life itself,*
> *This bubbling, restless force*
> *That churns inside us,*
>> *That seeks expression and direction*
>> *Like a rushing stream. . .*
>> *Sometimes formed by circumstances*
>> *As a stream is by its banks,*

But never contained by them.
Moving, changing form,
Ducking under obstacles, splashing over them. . .

My gift from God?
Life!
> *And how twice-gifted I am*
> *If the stream of my life has been given direction*
> *By the meaning of Jesus Christ.*

It sprouted quickly. . . but as it had no root, it withered away.

Matthew 13:6 NEB

Roots!
How can I put down my roots
In an age of such rapid change?
In a mobile society
Where friendships are transient,
And rules are changed before the ink is dry?

How can I put down my roots
When my children seldom see their grandparents,
When the world I knew as a child
No longer exists,
And the values which I was taught
Can no longer cope with a global community?

But I must have roots,
Or my strength will wither away!
My roots must be sent deep,
Down below the surface of social expectations,
Below the level of custom and culture,
Even deeper than friend and family and country . . .
My roots must go down to the being of God Himself.

. . . no pack for the road, no second coat, no shoes, no stick. . .
– Matthew 10:9, 10 NEB

No pack for the road,
No second coat . . .
    The constant conflict in life,
    To have,
    And to simplify.

      Something tells me that my effectiveness
      Operates in inverse ratio
      To my possessions,
         And yet my excuse for getting things
         Is that I may use them to be more effective.

      And the second coat I buy
      To keep me warm on life's journey,
         Turns out to be a burden over my shoulder
         Which slows my pace.

      Conflict!

Some men brought to him a paralytic, lying on a mat. Jesus . . . said to the paralytic,
"Take heart, son; your sins are forgiven."
— *Matthew 9:2*

A paralyzed man was brought to Jesus,
And Jesus forgave his sins.
Was that what he wanted?
Was that not a bit irrelevant,
A bit beside the point?

Not if we put it in different words.
A man came to Jesus,
Rigid with fear,
Unable to cope with life. . .
. . . and Jesus said to him,
Relax, friend,
You're all right.
God loves you, just the way you are.
He accepts you as His son.
Relax,
And put your feet on the ground,
And walk like a man.

I can believe that it worked.
I've seen it work.
That's what the gospel is all about.

The kingdom of heaven is like a mustard seed. . .
The kingdom of heaven is like yeast. . .
– Matthew 13:31, 33

In a world of well-packaged and slick
Products,
The ideas of the kingdom of heaven
Often seem a bit homemade and lumpy.

But Jesus never presented the ideas
Of the kingdom of heaven
As a finished product.
He pictured God's kingdom as raw material
Put into our hands.
The kingdom is a seed,
The kingdom is yeast,
The kingdom of heaven is people, not saints.
People growing,
Rising,
Working toward an ideal.
People not yet perfected,
But alive and moving.

And any packaging of the kingdom of heaven
Which gets too slick
Seems to lack that lumpy homemade quality
Of seeds and yeast.

Jesus took Peter, James, and John with him and led them up a high mountain,
where they were all alone.

– Mark 9:2

What busy person has not longed
For a quiet mountaintop somewhere,
An isolated hush of sky and tree
Where all the discordant sounds of life
    Would be far enough away
    To take on some harmony,
    Some sense of rhythm?

But sometimes
The only mountaintop experience that is allowed us
Is sitting on top of the mountain of things
That must be done.
    And there, without the magic hush of sky and tree,
    Can I find balance, and harmony?
        Anyone can have a sense of perspective
        At a distance,
        But it takes imagination
        To sort the large from the small
        Up close.

... the kingdom of heaven
is like a merchant looking for
fine pearls. . . . The kingdom
of heaven is like a net. . .
the fishermen pulled it up
on the shore . . . collected the
good fish in baskets,
but threw the bad away.
— *Matthew 13:45-48*

Sometimes
The kingdom of heaven and its objectives
Are clear and shining,
> *Like a pearl of great value.*
> *And though I must sell all I have to obtain it,*
> *I will,*
> *For I know what it is and what it costs.*

But when the kingdom of heaven
Gets to be like a net-full of fish,
Good,
Bad,
And indifferent,
Which I must sort out,
The going gets rough.
> *For it is not the cost that slows me up,*
> *But the indecision.*

What fools the nations are to
rage against the Lord. . .
"Come, let us break his chains,"
they say, "and free ourselves
from all this slavery to God."
— *Psalm 2:1-3 TLB*

Any conception of freedom
As breaking the forces which bind us to God
Is rebellion on a very shallow level.
> *Usually it is childish rebellion*
> *Against an immature understanding of God.*

Any deep understanding of God and life
Acknowledges that our freedom
Lies in our connectedness to God . . .
Not at the levels at which He has sometimes been
Institutionalized,
But at the level of life itself.

I cancelled all debt of yours because you begged me to. Shouldn't you have had
mercy on your fellow servant just as I had on you?
– Matthew 18:33

Sometimes I do not want to think of God
As being totally forgiving.
Because I do not want to totally forgive.

    I mean,
    If a person has done wrong
    He should be punished, shouldn't he?
    Else,
    Why should I bother to do right?
        God has laws, my reasoning goes,
        And if man breaks them,
        And God forgives and forgives,
        Why should the laws ever be kept?
        Of what validity are they?

But sometimes
A little bit of grace shines into my mind,
And I realize that the keeping and breaking of God's laws
Are their own punishment and reward,
        And anyone who has broken himself
        Against the law of God
        Needs all the forgiveness and love I can give him.

I sought the LORD and He answered me, and freed me from all my fears.

– Psalm 34:4 MLB

When I seek God,
And bring my concerns,
What will He say?
> *Will He give me the magic solutions,*
> *The instant answers,*
> *The guarantee to remove all troublesome things?*

Not always.
If this were so,
I would become weaker and weaker,
More dependent, and less of a person.

But when I seek God,
There is one sure promise . . .
> *He will help me to face up to the situation*
> *And free me from all my fears . . .*
>> *And when a situation is faced without fear,*
>> *It is no longer a problem.*
>> *It is an exciting experience.*

Jesus was angry as he looked around at them, but at the same time he felt sorry for them, because they were so stubborn and wrong.

– Mark 3:5 Good News for Modern Man

Being a Christian
Is sometimes a state of great frustration.
There are times when we glimpse the vastness
Of the potential
Contained in the Christian gospel,
> *And then one look around, or within,*
> *Can reveal what a tiny portion of this potential*
> *Is ever actualized,*
> *Or even comprehended.*

> > *And we squander our one short life*
> > *Not by any willingness to do evil,*
> > *But by becoming plodding persons*
> > *Who have lost sight of the wonder,*
> > > *And are caught up in taxes,*
> > > *The mortgage,*
> > > *The grocery bill,*
> > > *And setting the alarm clock,*
> > > *Ad nauseum . . .*

God,
Keep the dream alive in me!

God of truth, you hate those who serve worthless idols. . . .
– Psalm 31:6 TJB

God is central,
Living,
Life itself,
Unorganizable,
Moving, striking, creating.

Man constantly wants to organize God,
To build walls around Him,
To capture Him,
To project life toward Him,
To make God predictable, stagnant and deadly.

But what is true is true,
And those who worship God not as He is
But as they think He is,
Are only worshiping the creation of their own minds . . .
A worthless idol.

23

. . . For anyone who does not love his brother, whom he has seen,
cannot love God, whom he has not seen.
– 1 John 4:20

There was a time
When I thought an infidel
Was only defined as one who did not believe in God.
It was not until later
That I encountered the term infidelity
In reference to human relationships.

But now I wonder . . .
> *If I cannot keep faith with you*
> *Whom I see every day,*
>> *How could I possibly have faith in God*
>> *Whom I have not seen . . .*

>> *Or have I?*
>> *Does not the Spirit of God*
>> *Live in you?*

Let us fix our eyes on Jesus, the Pioneer and Perfecter of our faith . . .
– Hebrews 12:2

Who is that curious, ragged figure
Walking along the lonely seaside,
Sometimes by Himself,
Sometimes in the company of a few bedraggled men . . .
> *Could that be Jesus Christ,*
> *The man who has caused such change in the world*
> *These two thousand years?*

And where does He live?
Does He have a home in keeping with His greatness,
With chariots of the best sort parked outside?
> *I've heard it said*
> *He doesn't even have a place to rest His head.*

They tell me He's a man of ideas,
And Ideals,
That He has such a passion to teach and heal
That He forgets to eat and sleep.
> *Who is that curious, ragged figure?*
> *I wish He would disappear . . .*
> *He troubles me.*

Happy the man who cares for the poor and the weak:
if disaster strikes, Yahweh will come to his help.
–Psalm 41:1 TJB

It has been said
That the Good Lord looks after those
Who look after themselves.

But this is a deeper, more complex idea.
Those who win friendship by caring,
By being involved in the lives of others
Who apparently have nothing to give back,
*   May find that when disaster strikes,*
*   God will come to them,*
*   Possibly through the hands of the weak . . .*
*   The hands which they themselves*
*   Had helped to strengthen.*

But they did not understand what he meant and were afraid to ask . . .

– Mark 9:32

Learning
Takes great courage.
There is so much to learn about life
And God,
And the questions are so deep,
That it takes most of us our lifespan
Just to learn what the questions are.
    To have questions is a sign of wisdom,
    Not of stupidity.
    But so often we are afraid to ask the questions,
    Thinking everyone else but us
    Must know the answers . . .
And so we sit in our fearful silence,
And great questions are never asked.

How long shall I put up with you?
– Matthew 17:18

How long shall I put up with you?
These are words seldom spoken to a stranger.
> *They are spoken in the close bind*
> *Of interpersonal relationships.*

> *As a parent, how much longer must I put up with you,*
> > *You child with your lack of gratitude?*
> *As a child, how much longer must I put up with you,*
> > *You parent with your demands, your disapproval?*
> *As a wife, how much longer must I put up with you,*
> > *You husband with your irritating little habits?*
> *As a husband, how much longer must I put up with you,*
> > *You wife with your wants and complaints?*

How much longer must I put up with you?
Words spoken by Christ to His disciples, whom He loved.
Words always spoken by people who belong to each other,
People who are learning from each other what life is about
At close range.
> > *And the answer to the question is*
> > *That we must keep on putting up with each other's faults*
> > *As long as we want to keep on learning*
> > *All that there is to be learned*
> > *From each other.*

It is all right to be envious
If what I envy is worth envying.

> *But these desires,*
> *These things I want fiercely,*
> *Want so much that they obliterate the obstacles*
> *Encountered in obtaining them,*
> > *These wishes whose motivation springs*
> > *From my inner being . . .*
> > > *What are these I desire with all my heart?*

They are the things I will have.
And when I get them,
The sum of my life
Will only be worth what they are worth.
> *Are my desires, wishes and dreams*
> *Big enough to build a life on?*
> *Do I envy enough?*

They are in conflict with each other, so that you do not do what you want.

– *Galatians 5:17*

Most of us live with a double image.
There is the list of things we intend to do . . .
>   *Make that phone call,*
>   *Write that letter,*
>   *Take a walk with the children,*
>   *Do some good reading,*
>   *Say "I love you" more often,*
>   *Start a garden. . .*

And then there is the actual report of the day's actions . . .
>   *Walked past the phone all day and didn't call,*
>   *Didn't get the letter written yet,*
>   *Was too tired to take a walk,*
>   *Couldn't find a book,*
>   *Found fault with my family,*
>   *Decided to wait until next year to plant a garden . . .*

Is that what they call getting yourself put together,
To do what you really intended to do?

The word of Yahweh is integrity itself. . . .
– Psalm 33:4 TJB

The word of God
Is integrity itself . . .
  This speaks in part of the recorded word;
  But what about God's fresh word to us each day,
  Our living orders,
  Our immediate reactions,
  Our decision processes?

    Perhaps it would be helpful
    To invert the order of the words.
      Integrity itself *is the word of God,*
      God's word to us in every situation;
      A clean honesty which acts out of faith and love
      And not out of fear or hostility.

    Integrity in every situation.
    This is the word of God.
    These are our living orders.

For he has not despised or disdained the poor man in his poverty,
has not hidden his face from him. . . .
– Psalm 22:24 TJB

How unlike us!
We meet a man,
And judge him by his clothing,
    His speech,
    His education,
    His posture,
And secretly classify him as above or below us.
And although we may graciously relate to him
Or openly spurn him,
    The subtler workings of our hearts
    Often trick us into despising
    A man or woman
    Whom we consider to be of low standing.

    We are all born naked,
    And naked we return to our Maker.
    Any wealth or poverty is only a temporary condition . . .
        But to the person suffering poverty,
        It seems forever.
        If God has not hidden His face from the poor,
        How can he tell it?
            Is not my face sometimes the face of God to another,
            Accepting or rejecting him?

And why have you forced us to leave Egypt to bring us to this miserable location? It is no place for seed or fig trees, or vines, or pomegranates; there is not even any drinking water.

– Numbers 20:5 MLB

The Israelites crossing the desert
On the way to the promised land
Were indulging in humankind's favorite sport
Of looking back on the good old days,
> *Which, by the way, were not so good*
> *While they were being lived.*

God, how often I do that.
Moved by a great idea to go forward
Into some new promised land of human experience,
I go,
> *And then when the least inconvenience arises,*
> *I stand uncertain,*
> *Washed with waves of nostalgia*
> *For things that had given me pangs of frustration before.*

If I must remember,
Let me remember the slavery I left.
Let me remember the great idea,
> *And how good it feels to be hungry and clean*
> *And free.*

. . . what I have I give you.

– Acts 3:16

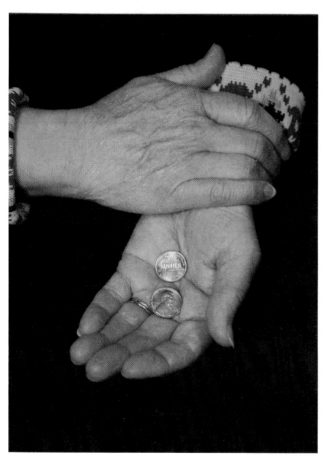

To say this,
And mean it,
Demands a totally new life-concept.

Somehow I tend to become possessive
Of things I consider strictly mine.
I hold on to my money,
        My home,
        My time,
        My love and concern.

Peter and John listened to Christ's words
Every day, for three years.
But it was only after the words had stopped,
And they began to experience
        'What I have I give you'
That they comprehended in any measure
What Jesus was talking about.

To test him, they asked him for a sign from heaven . . . He left them, got back into the boat and crossed to the other side of the lake.
– Mark 8:11, 13

If miracles happen in midair,
Exploding like fireworks in a dark sky,
    It is seldom when we ask for them.

But when people are hungry or sick,
Or lonely or troubled,
Or just bogged down with life,
    A person who cares and loves
    Can work miracles.

I cannot demand the power of the universe to be displayed
Because I am a child of God,
    And to the extent that I am aware
    Of the power within me,
    I will not need display.

37

Take note of what you hear . . .

– Mark 4:24 NEB

Every day, we hear.
We hear all that goes on around us. . .
> *The conversations, the musical sounds,*
> *The noise of the city or town,*
> *The traffic, the shops,*
> *The wind in the trees. . .*
But how often do we take note of what we hear?

Often we let the sounds slip by,
Unaware of their relationship to each other,
And to us.
We can learn by listening, and really hearing,
By taking note.
> *If we were to take this literally,*
> *And actually take notes on a whole day's hearing experience,*
> *What a rich day of learning we would discover!*

> *Listening for the voice of God*
> *In the sounds around us*
> *Might challenge the image we hold*
> *Both of God*
> *And of the world we live in.*

Now Joseph had a dream, and when he told it to his brothers, they only hated him
the more. . . but his father kept the saying in mind.
– Genesis 37:5, 11 RSV

How careful I must be
Not to kill the dreams of my children.

> *A young person may be a dreamer,*
> *Not even knowing the worth or meaning*
> *Of his own dreams.*
>> *Yet within him or her*
>> *There can be an awareness of great usefulness,*
>> *Somehow, somewhere.*

Joseph's dreams were of moons and stars
And shocks of corn,
And his father indulged him.
> *But if he had known that those dreams*
> *Would only be realized*
> *By suffering and pain and heartbreak,*
> *Would he have allowed Joseph to go on dreaming?*

Would I?

To Yahweh belong earth and all it holds, the world and all who live in it. . . .
– Psalm 24:1 TJB

The earth belongs to God,
And all who live in it . . .
    If we can have this concept in mind
    And affirm it in all our attitudes,
    Our outlook on life can be spared much of the fragmentation
    The Christian Church has traditionally experienced.

When we can believe that all is God's,
And that all goodness comes from God,
That all good is a sign of God's presence,
Then God is much more evident in His world.

    That none of us is totally good
    Nor totally evil
    Should not confuse the issue,
    But only clarify it.
        None of us is God,
        But we all belong to Him,
            And have responded in different ways.

        Finding a way to respond to God.
        Could that be the Christian message?

. . . a man with an evil spirit. . . no one could bind him anymore. . . . he tore the chains apart and broke the irons on his feet. No one was strong enough to subdue him.

– Mark 5:2-4

Is this the description of a free person?
A man with no controls,
A man who has broken all his restraints,
And thrown aside all his inhibitions?

No, this was a madman.
And the line between freedom and madness is thin.
For all the old restraints and inhibitions I discard,
There must be new ones,
Chosen in the free flow of the creative power
Of love,
Or my freedom will end in destruction.

The people who were in front and those who followed behind began to shout,
"Praise God! God bless him who comes in the name of the Lord!"
– Mark 11:9 TEV

If I am going to shout the current jargon,
And take up popular slogans,
Let me be sure I know what I am saying.

The Palm Sunday crowd
Were all ready to repeat the catchy words
Of the moment,
Shouting and waving Jesus on,
When they had not the slightest idea
What or whom they were cheering for. . .

. . . and when the cause came to a roaring crash
One week later,
Where were the jargon shouters,
The cloak spreaders?

They were still shouting the latest,
But the words had changed,
And this time they were saying,
Crucify Him,
Crucify Him!

. . . the evil men, who talk of peace to their neighbors while malice is in their hearts. . .

– Psalm 28:3 TJB

The evil men,
The bad guys. . .
> *Our definition of who they are*
> *And if they even exist in pure form*
> *Has shifted greatly.*

> *But one thing is sure;*
> *Persons who would think of themselves as honest*
> *Cannot have opposite motivations. . .*
> > > *Peace*
> > > *And malice.*

If we will have peace in the world
On a personal level
We cannot have dislike or hard feelings or hatred
Or prejudice toward any person,
No matter how unlikeable he may be.

> *If we cannot overcome our own private wars,*
> *How can we ever expect peace on a world scale?*

Indecency of any kind, or ruthless greed, must not so much as be mentioned among you, as befits the people of God.

– Ephesians 5:3 NEB

As expressions
Of the life of God,
We must be free to explore,
> *To be honest,*
> *To communicate with each other*
> *The struggles of our hearts,*
> *To ask questions.*
> *But those questions can never be*
> *The questions which would allow us to be*
> *Less than God created us to be.*
>> *Our ground rules*
>> *Should be lawful human behavior,*
>> *And our questions should be how,*
>> *As followers of Jesus Christ,*
>> *We can live extraordinarily creative*
>> *Warm, loving, and true*
>> *Human lives.*

The law of his God is in his heart; none of his steps shall slide.

– Psalm 37:31 KJV

The law of God in the heart . . .
For a Christian
This must be more than a set of words,
A right way
And a wrong way to do things.

It must be a kind of feeling
In the heart,
A kind of gentleness toward all men
And women,
A kind of respect which neither
Possesses others
Nor despises them,
A law which bends and adapts
And shapes to the occasion,
And always comes out acting
Like love.

At once Jesus realized that power had gone out from him. He asked, "Who touched my clothes?" his disciples answered, "You see the crowd crowding against you," "and yet you ask, 'Who touched me?' "

– Mark 5:30

It is a strange fact,
But some of the most important happenings
In our lives
Are not obvious to others.
>*The question you ask, which is important to you,*
>*May seem trivial,*
>*Or even less than intelligent*
>*To me,*
>*Because I do not understand the depth*
>*Of your wondering.*

The disciples thought Jesus had asked a foolish question. . .
In fact,
He was more perceptive than they.

>*How often do I misjudge the importance*
>*Of another's question?*

. . . do not worry. Nothing but evil can come of it. . . .
– Psalm 37:8 TJB

Worry
Is a strange thing.
We begin worrying about a certain circumstance
Or decision,
> *And the worry grows and becomes diffused*
> *Until it takes over our whole conscious*
> *And subconscious mind.*
>> *The worry itself*
>> *Can become so absorbing*
>> *That one can forget what the issue was*
>> *And begin to worry*
>> *About feeling so worried,*
>> *And to fear what worry can do. . .*
>>> *Until one becomes powerless*
>>> *To solve the original problem.*

How foolish!
If I can solve the problem,
Let me get to work and do something about it.
> *If it is beyond me,*
> *Let me hand it over to God.*

Therefore, since the promise of entering his rest still stands, let us be careful that none of you be found to have fallen short of it.

– Hebrews 4:1

Rest . . .
What does the word rest mean to me?
    At six o'clock in the morning
    When the alarm tears into my sleep,
    Rest would be heaven!

But short of sleeping all day,
What kind of rest do I want?
    Obviously, while I'm living,
    I'm not thinking of final rest.
    While life lasts,
    What definition of rest do I crave?

I do not want a rest which allows me to waste
precious days of life,
A complacency which tells me that nothing really matters,
    But rather, a rest which tells me
    That under all the restlessness and wondering
    There is purpose.
        There is the underlying Spirit of God
        Interlocking all life
        In a oneness of meaning.

Beloved.
There is a secure feeling about that word.
When a person is be-loved,
It is a special kind of being.
 It is being—love-ed.
 It is a past, present, future kind of a word
 That surrounds one with a warmth and comfort
Nothing can break or mar.
  The faults of a beloved person
  Are smiled at by the person who loves,
  And the ordinary virtues
  Seem good out of all measure.

To be beloved
Is the rarest and most beautiful of gifts.
 To be beloved of God
 Should be enough to make a saint of anyone!

And Isaac . . . was gathered unto his people, being old and full of days . . .
– Genesis 35:29 KJV

God,
When I looked in the mirror this morning,
I realized I'm middle-aged.
>*It seems impossible. . .*
>*I've always been so young.*

>*But here I am,*
>*In the middle of my life,*
>*Standing between the generations,*
>>*Robbed of the illusions of youth*
>>*And not yet given the serenity of age.*

>*I'm restless, God.*
>*What do You want of me?*
Perhaps You want of me what I want most of myself . . .
Let me sit quietly and think about those things for a while.

I'm only half-full of days, God.
Help me to live the rest of them
With an awareness of their value.

At midday darkness fell over the whole land . . .
and Jesus cried aloud, ". . . why hast thou forsaken me?"

– Mark 15:33, 34 NEB

Darkness,
And a feeling of being forsaken by God. . .
How common these are to our human existence.
> *Yet how ironic it is*
> *That the very times when the sky is darkest*
> *The greatest battles are being fought,*
>> *And when we think we have been forsaken by God*
>> *He is there all the time,*
>>> *Struggling to create within us*
>>> *That which could not be created*
>>> *Except by*
>>> *Pain.*

In darkness and struggle
We are far from being forsaken by God. . .
> *In fact,*
> *Only then are we involved*
> *In the cosmic struggle at its deepest.*

Fresh skins for new wine . . .

Mark 2:22 NEB

Awareness
Is a troublesome thing.
It is not an
Off-again, on-again,
Take-it-or-leave-it state of affairs.

> *A new awareness of Life*
> *Is like a whole new blend of ingredients,*
> *Rising up,*
> *Sparkling,*
> *Pushing its way to greater power.*
>> *And even if we ever so politely*
>> *And gently*
>> *Concede*
>> *To try to house it in old containers,*
>> *It will someday*
>> *Explode.*

They that wait upon the Lord shall renew their strength;
they shall mount up with wings as eagles; they shall run
and not be weary, they shall walk and not faint.

– Isaiah 40:31 KJV

They had gathered in the church for half an hour
Before the traditional worship service . . .
    Two rows of fresh-faced young people,
    With a few up front playing guitars.
        And there were others
        Scattered quietly in the pews.
        A balding middle-aged man,
        A bit thick above the belt,
            And an older lady
            With pearl earrings and a pink hat,
            Singing an octave lower.

All so different.
And yet as they sang,
There was something alike about their faces,
A kind of longing . . .
    A youth that was not chronological years,
    But a refusal to let dreams die,
        And a willingness,
        Even at the risk of sounding foolish,
        To find fresh ways of expressing those dreams.

Anyone who has seen me has seen the father. . . .
– John 14:9

At times I have wondered
If God is a form,
Or if He is a great faceless power,
A creative force . . .
    And the question troubles me in the abstract.

And then I remember that He once took on the form
Of a man,
With a face and hands.

    Now I walk along the street
    And look into eyes. . . .
    I see so many eyes for God to smile in,
    So many hearts for God to cry in,
    So many minds for God to think in,
        That I wonder again
        If He needs a form of His own.
        Perhaps this is the part of Himself
        That He has given to us.
        Perhaps we are the form He takes.

    Perhaps we are the faces of God.

They love sacrifice: they sacrifice flesh and eat it. . .

– Hosea 8:13 RSV

Our motives. . .
How complex they can become!
    We begin doing a thing because it is right,
    And end up wondering
    What it will cost us
        Or what it will pay.

If only we could carry through our good impulses,
Our God impulses,
With the same quality in which they were conceived,
How filled with the pure joy of creation
Our lives would be!

... reports about Jesus reached the ears of Prince Herod. "This is John the Baptist,"
he said . . . "John has been raised to life."
– Matthew 14:1 NEB

A thing done long ago,
Repressed,
Covered over,
Practically forgotten . . .
    And then there is the name,
        The name of Jesus Christ
        And the values for which it stands,
        The name which shines across my mind
        Like a searchlight,
            Showing up the smallness and meanness
            Which has been stuffed down
            And covered up.

Sometimes I hear that name . . .
And instead of conjuring up a mental image
Of the lovely Jesus, meek and mild,
    A disturbing thing can happen.
    My private can of worms comes tumbling open,
    And whatever it was that troubled me deeply
    Comes crawling out.
        "Christ?" said Herod,
        "Yikes! That's John the Baptist,
        Whose head I cut off!"

Yahweh . . . I am your guest, and only for a time . . .
– Psalm 39:12 TJB

We are accustomed
To some word pictures . . .
> *We are strangers in the world,*
> *We are pilgrims*
> *Taking a long journey to the beyond.*
All these portray not only a feeling of the
Temporary nature of life,
But also a disinterest in the surroundings
As we pass through.

> *But the idea of being a*
> *"Guest of God"*
> *Intrigues me.*
> *A guest, although he will not stay forever,*
> *Is concentrating on the place where he is.*
> *He is aware of its sights and sounds,*
> *Delighted by its wonders,*
> *And ready to make the most of each day.*

> *I would like to live*
> *As a guest of God*
> *In this world.*

A sense of awe was everywhere, and many marvels and signs were brought about. . . .

– Acts 2:43 NEB

Two days
Can be so different,
Two days lived by the same person,
In the same circumstances.
    One day is alive,
    Full of significance.
    Things move us to laugh or cry,
    To feel pleasure or pain.
        The other day is dead,
        With no particular meaning.
        We feel unable to sing or laugh,
        To care at all whether pain or pleasure
        Exist.

Usually the outward motions we go through
Are the same,
And nobody knows.
    But what makes the difference?

        For me it is the sense of awe that comes over me
        When I remember
        That simply to be alive
        Is a miracle.

And the name of Jesus, by awakening faith, has strengthened this man.
– Acts 3:16 NEB

I get lost in it . . .
    The social injustice,
    The prejudice,
    The religious divisions,
        The subtle snobberies by which men kill
        Each other,
        And me, if I try to care.

And I say, God, I know the world's a mess.
I love it, but I hate some of its situations.
I know something should be done,
But don't expect me to bat my one soft head against a brick wall.
I'll get hurt. My children will get hurt.
And what good will it do?

        And then, through the fog,
        I get a glimpse of Jesus Christ,
        A lonely figure, out there ahead,
        Walking where I dare not walk,
        Doing what I dare not do.

        I put my head down and think,
        Torn between the desire to follow,
        And the instinct to play it safe . . .
            He did it.
            Do I dare?

The fool hath said in his heart, there is no God.
– Psalm 53:1 KJV

The debate goes on . . .
Is God dead, or isn't He?
It was on the front of Time magazine,
And that makes it official, doesn't it?
> *Sorry about your God, say the bumper stickers,*
> *Mine's not dead.*
> *I talked to Him this morning in Miami,*
> *Said a reliable source,*
> *And He was alive and well!*

And so we banter on,
Dealing with absurdities, superficialities,
And outmoded concepts,
Wondering what it would be like if God were dead
And out of the way,
And yet horrified at the prospect.

> *Perhaps the whole uproar did us all good.*
> *Perhaps we did get rid of the white-bearded God*
> *Who sat on a cloud in His bathrobe,*
> > *And have come closer to understanding His true greatness.*

> *I live, and you live,*
> *And the whole Universe throbs with life and beauty.*
> *How could God possibly be dead?*

Everyone who fears Yahweh will be taught the course a man should choose.
– Psalm 25:42 TJB

As a person
Given the gift of life
There is one thing I must fear,
>   *And that is participating in the destruction*
>   *Of my life*
>   *Or the lives of others.*

>   *Fear is a word which we instinctivly dislike.*
>   *We do not like to fear anything or anyone.*
>   *But fear. . . fear of spoiling what is beautiful. . .*
>   *Can have a healthy use as well.*
>   *It can become a kind of sensitivity*
>   *Which warns us of coming obstacles and dangers,*
>   *Which makes us turn away from certain practices*
>   *And attitudes,*
>   *Because they send back the wrong impulses.*

>   *Perhaps a better word for it is respect.*
>   *By fear/respect*
>   *I am able to choose a positive course.*

He saw that they were in serious trouble, rowing hard and struggling
against the wind and waves.
– Mark 6:48 TLB

Why does man so often find himself
The enemy of nature?
> *In Jesus we see something else.*
> *He was a person who had a complete knowledge*
> *Of who He was,*
>> *Who He was in relationship to God,*
>> *And to His fellow-man.*

>> *But something which leaves me fragmented*
>> *And thrown back on*
>> *Faith-without-understanding,*
>> *Is Christ's ability to walk on water,*
>> *Or multiply bread . . .*
>>> *. . . His astounding relationship*
>>> *To the world of matter.*

Were these only tales, told by superstitious fishermen,
Or do they challenge our minds with some mystery?

If I could claim such a complete awareness of God and man
As Christ had,
What would my relationship be to the world of matter?
Who knows?

From strength to strength,
From high to high,
> *This is how we would like life to be,*
> *Without going through the lows*
> *And plains between.*

Sometimes our short memory is a curse,
Sometimes it is a mercy.
> *When we are feeling high on life*
> *We wonder what is the matter with the rest*
> *Of the stupid, mixed-up human race,*
>> *And then suddenly we feel stupid and mixed-up*
>> *Ourselves,*
>> *And we know.*

But when I can believe, whether I can feel it or not,
That the Spirit of God lives in me,
I can make it, with some sense of balance,
Through the proud highs
And the desperate lows.

He said to her, ". . . it is not fair to take the children's bread and throw it to the dogs."
"Sir," she answered, "Even the dogs under the table eat the children's scraps."
– Mark 7:27, 28 NEB

Jesus threw a prejudiced statement
At a Greek woman,
A woman whom His people considered a dog,
An untouchable.
>   *He must have done it tongue-in-cheek*
>   *To see if she would accept*
>   *This evaluation of herself.*

>   *And when she responded with satirical wit,*
>   *Jesus Christ was overjoyed.*
>   *He considered her sense of humor*
>   *Great faith!*

God, I could do with a little of that.
Sometimes when my ability to believe in people fails me,
At least give me a sense of humor
To see through the little webs we tangle ourselves in.

But. . . he spoke to them:
"Take heart! It is I;
do not be afraid. . . ."
At this they were
completely dumbfounded.
– *Mark 6:50 NEB*

In the midst of life's most shattering
And terrifying circumstances,
We want to turn our heads away,
To look up and beyond for help from God.

> *But then there comes a voice from the middle of the trouble,*
> *Even from the thing which caused our fear,*
> *Saying, Fear not, for it is I.*

> *And we are dumbfounded*
> *That the thing we feared most*
> *Must be taken into ourselves*
> *To bring peace.*
>> *And the fear leaves,*
>> *But the pain stays*
>> *And changes into wonder,*
>>> *Choking us with the nearness of this power*
>>> *We thought so far away.*

Is there a ghost walking on your sea?
Reach out and touch it.
You may find the living Christ.

The Lord God hath spoken, who can but prophesy?

– Amos 3:8 KJV

It comes at me,
Not by angels and the sound of trumpets,
But through events and circumstances,
This voice of God.

And when it comes,
I must be able to recognize
What is truth in a given situation.

And having recognized truth
I must be willing to speak it,
Even if I am the one who will have to change most
Because I have spoken.

But God,
That's not what You told me yesterday!
Yesterday's word was for yesterday,
My child.
This is today.

His purpose was to create in himself one new man out of two, thus making peace, and in the one single body to reconcile both of them to God through the cross, by which he put to death their hostility.

– *Ephesians 2:16*

The cross
Was meant to be a sign of peace,
A sign that the wars were over,
The barriers were down,
And men of differing opinions could accept each other.
　　　Jesus Christ died for that,
　　　To take down the walls.

Among other things,
His death was a powerful demonstration
Against the ugliness of prejudice,
Of religious rightness and bigotry.

　　　God, I have to be careful
　　　That I don't take that same cross,
　　　That sign of peace,
　　　And hold it in front of me as a barrier,
　　　As a weapon,
　　　As a wall,
　　　And negate everything it stands for.

"The Son of Man is going to be betrayed into the hands of men, They will kill him, and on the third day he will be raised to life." And the disciples were filled with grief.
– Matthew 17:22, 23

The paradox of Easter. . .
    We mourn the crucifixion
    And celebrate the resurrection,
        Yet how could one have been
        Without the other?

The paradox of our lives. . .
    We hope for the beauty of a new awareness,
    And fear the uncertainty and risk
    Of losing everything
    To find ourselves.
        Yet how can we have one
        Without the other?

As I live, says the Lord, what you have said in my hearing, I will do to you.
– Numbers 14:28 RSV

Do our words shape the course of our lives?

> *I can look around me*
> *And see causes as worthless,*
> *People as useless,*
> *Myself as a failure,*
> *And everything as futile,*
>> *And that is the way the world,*
>> *At least my private world,*
>> *Will be.*

But if I can look at the same set of circumstances
> *And find something affirming,*
> *Something to say Bravo about,*
> *Some bit of blind faith that will let me*
>> *Believe the best about myself*
>> *And others,*
>> *Will these things not turn out*
>> *To be what my life is about?*

It's not a case of magic.
It's a simple fact.
What I see, and hear, and speak,
I become.

Remember those in prison as if you were there with them. . .
– Hebrews 13:3 NEB

"With. . ."
What a difference that word can make
In our attitude toward our brother.
>   *I'm not for you,*
>   *I'm with you.*
>   *I'm a part of you, and all that happens to you.*

If you are in prison,
I feel compelled to search my mind to understand
What hunger and confusion of heart
Caused you to strike out and offend society,
>   *Offend yourself.*
>   *And why you have come to be judged as guilty*
>   *When so many guilty men go free. . .*
>   *When no man is totally innocent. . .*
>   *When I am not innocent. . .*

>   *And I find myself in your prison.*
>   *For while one of us is bound,*
>   *How can any of us be free?*

"What shall I do, then, with Jesus who is called Christ?" Pilate asked.

– Matthew 27:22

Sometimes
We are in honest doubt
As to what to do.
    But other times we run about
    Asking this person and that person,
        What shall I do?
        What shall I do?
    When we know perfectly well
    What should be done.
        But still we ask,
        Hoping we will hear
        Not what we should hear
        But what we wanted to hear.
    For most of us know what we should do,
    But few of us have the courage to do it.

". . . you are Peter, and on this rock I will build my church. . ."
Jesus turned and said to Peter, "Out of my sight, Satan! You are a stumbling block
to me."

– Matthew 16:18, 23

To set up ourselves
Or anyone else
As having a perfect knowledge of God,
As being revered and holy,
Is foolish.

Like Peter,
We all have inspired glimpses of God,
And there are moments when we stand spiritually tall.
But the next moment
We may be so insensitive
That we not only misunderstand God ourselves
But cause someone else to fall
Flat on his face.

Rocks and stumbling blocks
Are made of the same stuff.

Peter said to Jesus . . . (He did not know what to say . . .)
A voice came . . . "Listen . . .!"
– Mark 9:5-7

Peter sounds like someone I know well.
The more unsure he was,
The more he talked.
> *And when he talked,*
> *Merely to fill the disturbing silence,*
> *He usually said silly or even harmful things.*

When I am unsure,
If I could only learn to listen to the silence,
And find there a wiser voice,
I would have fewer regrets.

" . . . and as he was not one of us, we tried to stop him."
– Mark 9:38 NEB

He is not one of us . . .
What an admission of alienation from a human being!
   Who is not one of us?
   Are we not all one creation?
     When I begin to pick out those
     Who are not my kind,
     The list grows and grows
       Until I find myself in a very lonely
       And alienated corner,
         Possessive of a few people
         Whose worth hinges on their loyalty
         To me
         And my way.

In the New Testament
The enemies of Christ were not the sinners.
They were the righteous
Who thought they knew it all.

When reading Paul's account of his life,
His certainty on the subject
Of his rightness
Is almost startling.
>   *Two thousand years later,*
>   *We have different data from which to draw,*
>   *And may come, in our culture,*
>   *To some different conclusions than Paul did.*

But one thing is outstanding about this man.
He assessed the situation,
Drew on the spirit of God within him,
Made decisions,
And lived by them.
>   *And somehow,*
>   *His life had tremendous value to himself*
>   *And others.*

"We have left everything to follow you! What then will there be for us?"
– Matthew 19:27 NIV

Peter
Was so like us.
He grandly left everything for the sake of Christ,
And then wondered what he was going to get
Out of being a disciple.

   And we . . .
   We follow Christ.
   What will there be in it for us?
      Will it mean years of tramping about
      Doing small and seemingly isolated deeds of love,
      Traveling dusty roads,
      And making friends with the wrong people,
      Incurring the wrath of those who cannot see God anew,
      And ending up on a cross?
That is what was in it for Christ Himself.
Will we still follow?

"Lord, are you at this time going to restore the kingdom to Israel?"
– Acts 1:6

The disciples had goals for Christ.
They wanted Him to deliver a certain people
At a certain time
From the hands of their oppressors.

Jesus Christ had wider goals.
He dreamed of delivering all mankind
For all time
From the oppression they suffered at their own hands,
From the fear,
And guilt,
And lack of love that made their lives small
And pinched, and unfree.

They walked with Him every day,
Ate the same food,
Saw the same sun rise every morning . . .
But they perceived things differently.
And how do I perceive life?
Are my expectations too small
For the mind of Christ?

81

That is why we struggle and work hard,
because we have placed
our faith in the living God.
– 1 Timothy 4:10 TEV

To believe in God as living,
As living in the persons around me,
Is no easy faith.
    It is hard work,
    And a constant test of my integrity
    To be so closely confronted
    By God
    In every activity of life.

    But that sense of living
    So close to the core of life
    Is worth all the struggle.

And Balak said to Balaam, "Come now, I will take you to another place; perhaps it will please God that you may curse them for me from there."
– Numbers 23:27 RSV

Balaam!
How I detest his spinelessness,
And identify with him all at once,
Trying to manipulate circumstances
In the name of God,
And collect the fee.

Unless I can make my decisions in life
Strictly clear of what they will get me or cost me,
In terms of dollars and cents,
I cannot claim to be letting the clear channel
Of God's creative power
Flow through me.
What I decide in the best of conscience
May turn out to my financial advantage.
Bravo!
But if I decide
With my ear on the heart,
And my eye on the pot,
How can I expect anything but confusion?

The only thing that counts is faith expressing itself through love.
– *Galatians 5:6*

The values of love
Are hard to come by,
Hard to define,
And hard to ever arrive at.
    Yet somewhere in the nonbeing
    There is a state of rightness
    Known only to the heart
    Of the individual believer.
        Faith in God,
        Active in love for those around him.

        When we do not have it
        It is the thing we seek most,
        And when we have it,
        We know that it is the only thing
        Which really matters.

But Moses' hands grew weary; so . . . Aaron and Hur held up his hands, one on one side, and the other on the other side; so his hands were steady until the going down of the sun.
– Exodus 17:12 RSV

The battle had been a long one,
And Moses' hands, held up over the people,
Began to tremble.
He needed help.
> *And here I sit,*
> *With my little pile of worries*
> *Clutched in my fists,*
> *Clutched so tightly that my hands are useless.*

Moses had two friends come and hold his hand up.
Do I have two friends,
Just two,
Who would come and do that for me?
> *Are there two friends I have helped*
> *When their hands were full*
>> *or tired,*
>> *Or knotted in anxiety?*
>>> *No?*
>>> *Then who can I call?*

Can you not see, you quibbler, that faith divorced from deeds is barren?

– James 2:21 NEB

Barren,
Unable to reproduce itself,
Sterile . . .
    That is a fitting description of a faith in God
    Which depends wholly on creeds and doctrines and dogmas
    For its validity.

    It is too clean, too compact,
    Too fossilized.
        It belongs in a museum
        Behind glass doors that say do not touch,
        Pickled in formaldehyde.

Things that grow
Are damp and smelly.
They spring up from the dirt, cultivated by red, wet worms.
They are conceived in joy, and born in pain.
    Things that are alive grow up and face the wind,
    A little bent, perhaps, but alive,
    Sometimes defying all reasons why.
        And God can never be very far from things
        That are alive,
        For He is Life itself!

"Master, we are sinking. Do you not care?" He awoke . . . and said to the sea,
"Hush, be still!" . . . "Why are you such cowards?"
– Mark 4:39, 40 NEB

This is an interesting mixture of commands
To the sea and the disciples.
 The roar of the sea,
 The panicky calls of the men
 All seemed a part of the general confusion.

But it only took one voice,
One man who was in tune with both man and his environment
To stand up with fearless courage,
And there was a calm.

There is a secret in this story
Which is taking us thousands of years
To comprehend.

Then the priest . . . shall be unclean until the even.
– Numbers 19:7 KJV

Involvement in life
Often leaves me with a bad taste in my mouth.
I must rub shoulders with a man
Whose values are not mine.
I see a play,
And the ethic or lack of ethic displayed in it
Leaves me frustrated and in despair.
I trust people, and they make me out to be a fool,
I believe in people, and they do stupid things,
Or someone believes in me,
And I let him down.
How simple it would be to go back to an abstract belief
Where I could read the Bible and pray,
And let it all take care of itself . . .
But this way,
With God living in me,
The only way I can worship is to get involved in life,
Which, although it is sacred,
Is no lily-white affair.

I pray also that the eyes of your heart may be enlightened. . . .

– Ephesians 1:18

There come low points in life
When we are tempted to ask,
    Is that all there is?
        Getting up in the morning,
        Rushing to school or to work,
        Doing household chores,
            Fighting to get enough money
            To pay the bills and the taxes,
                Worrying about the drip in the roof
                And the children's teeth,
                    And trying not to get fat
                    And bald,
                    And baggy-eyed?
                        Is this all there is?

Close your eyes and think,
And you'll know it's not.
    There are other eyes behind your everyday eyes,
    That can see beyond the tangle of circumstances.
    An inner glow,
    A second sight,
    Something that not only makes sense of it all,
    But gives life a sense of holiness.

And God said . . . and it was so.
– Genesis 1:24

And God said,
And it was so.
The simple, powerful Genesis story of man's beginnings.

But that was in the beginning,
And much has happened since the beginning.
    Now,
    Given the power of life
    In these human containers,
        Who creates the world we live in?
        Who creates its values,
        Its pressures,
        Its judgments,
        Its standards,
            Its ability to accept or reject,
            To build or destroy?

You say,
And I say,
And it is so.
The shape of the world is created
By our words.

And we know that all things
work together for good
to them that love God.

– *Romans 8:28*

God, I've gone as far as I can go,
And now I'm stymied.
I have this perfectly beautiful set of plans laid out . . .
Why don't You answer my prayers,
And make it all happen? Why?

Of course, I do remember last month
When I had a different set of plans
I was impatient to implement.
I can see now that they would have been a disaster.
And last year I was knocking on doors
That never opened,
Until a great one effortlessly opened for me,
And two years ago I was trying
To force an issue
Which I'm thankful now never happened.

But this time, God,
Take it from me!
This one is really a good idea.
Why don't You make things move?

Faith
And a good conscience
Are the only workable combination
In any form of belief.

Faith is the inner response,
The unseeing belief that somewhere, somehow
There is a God.
> *But when it all becomes very real,*
> *And I find that God living in the lives*
> *Around me,*
> People,
> > *The only thing which can validate that faith*
> > *Is a good conscience*
> > *In regard to my human relationships.*

And that takes more than retreating for prayers.

Tell the next generation that God is here. . . .
– Psalm 48:14 TJB

What can we tell our children about God?
Our knowledge is so imperfect,
Our faith so faltering,
Our lives so inconsistent,
Our understanding of the Eternal so fragmentary . . .
    What can we teach them about God?

    There is one thing we can say with assurance,
    And that is,
    "God is here . . ."
        God is here,
        In your today and in your tomorrows.
        Go and find Him in every place,
        And recognize the world as His.
            God is here.
            Go and listen, and look, and feel,
            And learn what that means
            In your own terms.

The seed that fell into good soil is the man
who hears the word and understands it,
who accordingly bears fruit . . .
– Matthew 13:23 NEB

The person who hears
And understands God's word
Is the man who will bear fruit;
 And the amount of fruit he bears
 Will not be in proportion
 To the number of times he hears,
  But to the number of times
  He understands what he has heard.

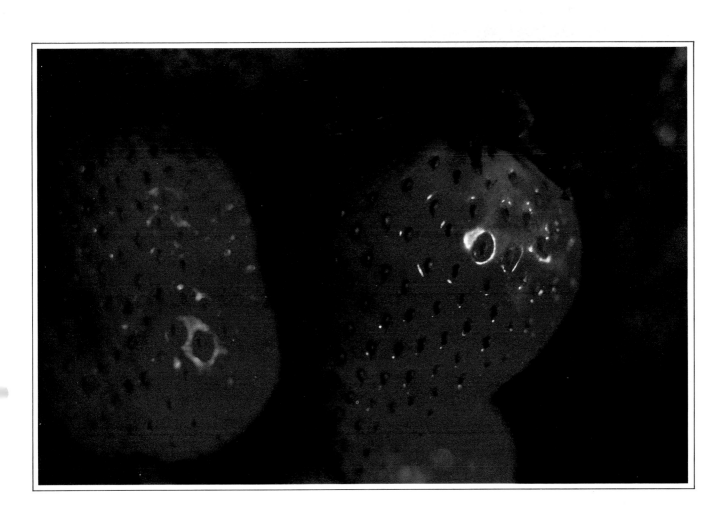

God, we have heard with our own ears . . . of the deeds you performed . . . in days long ago. . . . Yet now you abandon and scorn us. . . .
– Psalm 44:1, 9 TJB

The whole gist of this Psalm,
Sung as a national lament,
*   Is that God just isn't*
*   What He used to be.*

The past was great,
And God was there.
But who can bear the present?

*   It isn't fair.*
*   We're losing all the games,*
*   And we're playing just as well as ever . . .*
*   We're just as honest,*
*   As loving,*
*   As truthful,*
*   As eager in our search for the right as we ever were,*
*   But somehow we're still losing.*

*   It isn't fair, God!*

Yahweh is near to the broken-hearted, he helps those whose spirit is crushed.
– Psalm 34:18 TJB

If God is near to the brokenhearted,
Then those who know the experience of being broken
Are near to God . . .
> *Not only broken for one's own hurts,*
> *But, in a wider expanse of consciousness,*
> *Broken for the state of the world*
> *And mankind.*

To feel the hurts of the world
As a personal hurt
> *Makes one feel at the same time*
> *Forsaken of God,*
> *And very near to God.*
>> *It makes one feel both broken in heart,*
>> *And yet nearer to the center of wholeness,*
>> *Yahweh.*

Is it some kind of universal law,
That I must break out of my own separate heart
Before I can become a part of the great heart
Of God?

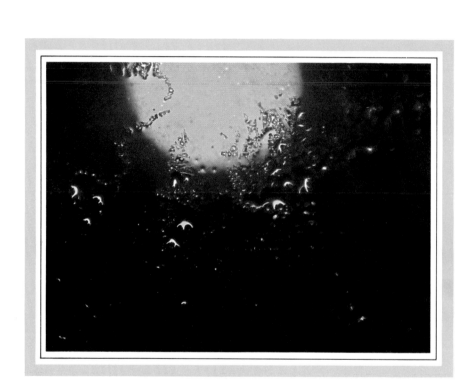

As surely as the coming of dawn
or the rain of early Spring. . . .
– Hosea 6:3 TLB

Sometimes we may be so demanding
In our search for meaning,
For purpose,
Even for God,
That we do not have the quietness of heart to know
He is near.
> *To think of the presence of God*
> *As an inescapable fact*
> *Is a relief.*
> > *To know that God is there,*
> > *As surely as the dawn,*
> > *That He will flow into our spirits*
> > *As surely as the rain falls on the earth . . .*

This knowledge takes away the demanding
And brings peace.

For lo, he who forms the mountains, and creates the wind, and declares
to man what is his thought. . . .
— *Amos 4:13 RSV*

Sometimes I am overpowered by the meaning
Of a single life . . .
    My life,
    Your life.

    On an ordinary day,
    A feeling of tremendous significance
    Can come over me,
        Significance glimpsed from the shape
        Of cattails in the swamp,
        The smoothness of new-fallen snow,
        Or the line of the mountain against the sky . . .

    What is the origin of such thoughts,
    And why do I, as a person, think them?

When the wonder of being a person
Crosses with the wonder of there being a God,
    The thoughts of mankind seem to take on an
    Extra dimension.

Happy the man . . . whose spirit is incapable of deceit!

– Psalm 32:1, 2 TJB

Incapable . . .
Is it good to be incapable of doing anything?

Yes!
It is good to be incapable of hurting another
For the sake of one's own pride.
It is good to be incapable of fooling oneself
As to one's own importance.

It is good to be incapable
Of living without honesty,
Clean-burned to the core,
Able to know,
And yet to accept and go on,
Not covering up and pretending,
But realizing,
And wishing toward more truth.

It is good to be incapable
Of settling for anything
But the hardest,
Truest,
And best.

. . . and the love you have, each for all
and all for each, grows ever greater.

– 2 Thessalonians 1:3 NEB

Growing
Is seldom a graceful process.
It is shoots and half-formed leaves,
Big teeth and bony knees.
Growing is the process of something
Becoming larger, taller,
More mature.

   And although growing
   Is not always a graceful process,
   Poised and polished and finished,
   It is preferable to its alternative . . .

For when a plant or animal or person
Or mind or spirit
Stops growing,
It begins the process of dying.

Women again must dress in becoming manner . . .
not decked out with . . . expensive clothes, but with good deeds. . . .
– 1 Timothy 2:9, 20 NEB

As a woman,
I don't think I'd get far
Walking down the street
Dressed only in my good deeds,
> *Paul to the contrary notwithstanding.*

But there is a truth about these words
Which is real.
When life is empty for me,
I become obsessed with the externals . . .
> *Clothing*
> *And housing*
> *And "what shall we have for dinner?"*
>> *But when there are rich relationships with others,*
>> *When life is filled with a sense of giving,*
>> *Of contributing in some way to the world,*
>> *Any old pair of jeans will do!*
>> *What does it matter?*

A false witness will not go unpunished, and he who utters lies will not escape.
– Proverbs 19:5 RSV

The man or woman who subscribes to a lie
Will not be free.
Lies and freedom cannot coexist;
Only truth and freedom are compatible.
   I cannot be free,
   Living in my own lies,
   Or living out the lies of others.

But what is true?
   Whatever makes me free to be
   The person I was created to be,
   Unchained,
   An authentic creation of God,
      These are true,
      And the opposites are lies.

A free life is a true life . . .
And that is not as irresponsible as it may sound.

> "You think as men think, not as God thinks."
> – *Mark 8:33 NEB*

When Peter heard all the trouble
That was to come to Jesus,
He begged Him to avoid it at any cost,
Even if it meant losing the central meaning of His life.

    But Jesus said,
    Your thoughts are destructive, Peter,
    Not creative.
        The creative power in man knows
        That certain values are to be followed,
        Even if they bring on seeming disaster,
        For they are the basic stuff of life
        And are indestructible.

        But it was hard for Peter,
        As it is hard for us,
        To understand that the greatest disaster
        Is for a man to save his skin
        And lose his soul.

Let our God come . . . Preceding him, a devouring fire, round him, a raging storm. . . .
– Psalm 50:3 TJB

Somehow,
We cannot think of upset
> *And upheaval*
> *And unrest*
> *As being the doings of God.*
We equate God and peace.
We want to get away from trouble,
And back to God.

> *But sometimes*
> *God's working in a situation*
> *Seems like a devouring fire*
>> *And a raging storm.*
>> *And the creative wind that blows*
>> *From winter's ice to summer's flowers*
>> *May sweep us off our feet,*
>> *And leave us, foolishly,*
>> *Angry at the wind.*

"The word is near you;
it is in your mouth and in your heart";
that is, the word of faith we are proclaiming.
– Romans 10:8

This morning the pastor stood up and said,
"Hear the word of the Lord."
> *And then he started to read a story*
> *Out of the New Testament*
> *About people*
> *Going about their everyday lives*
> *With no idea*
> *That the story of their doings*
>> *Would be read to future generations*
>> *As the word of God.*

And what about us?
Do we have a sense of living
That which may someday be passed on
As tradition,
> *Or even inspiration?*

Your hand will unmask all your enemies . . . Yahweh will engulf them in his anger . . .
you will wipe their children from the earth. . . .
– Psalm 21:8-10 TJB

This frame of mind
Has caused much evil.
>> *The idea that my cause is just*
>> *And my enemies are God's enemies*
>>> *Builds up righteous hatred*
>>> *Which can cause atrocities*
>>> *In the name of a just*
>>> *Or even religious*
>>> *Cause.*

Is this not the frame of mind
Christ tried to break?
>> *Love,*
>> *The greatest sorter of values,*
>> *Will not allow us to pray to God*
>> *For the destruction of another,*
>>> *Much less for the destruction*
>>> *Of all his innocent descendants.*

Such thinking
Is pre-Christian.

If anyone would come after me, he must . . . take up his cross daily and follow me.
– Luke 9:23

As Christians,
We are to take up a cross
And follow Christ.
    But what is that cross,
    That heaviness laid across our shoulders?

It is caring,
When being careless of another would be easier.

It is daring to love,
In a world where love is laughed at,
        Where it is taken as softness
        And a bit naive.

It is daring to give
                And trust and share,
                When getting
                And suspecting
                And keeping what is yours
                Are the sensible things.

Taking up your cross and following Christ
Means being just a little foolish
In a world of practical people.
It means being a beautiful fool.

Create in me a clean heart, oh God;
and renew a right spirit within me.
– Psalm 51:10 KJV

Is creation a word which happened once,
And it was done,
Or does God continue to create?
> *Is created life a set pattern*
> *Which is passed blindly from generation to generation,*
>> *Or does it change in the passing*
>> *So that even as it goes it changes form*
>> *And creates new ways of being?*

Creation . . .
God, who created,
May continue to create.
> *And if I stand still, unchanging,*
> *I may find myself out of the flow*
> *Of that creation.*

I may think I have a watertight theology,
But what happens to it when I confront life?
    Does it leave me stranded and self-righteous,
    Hating the crowd,
    Or does it give me a basis for loving the world
    As God loves it?

Truth, mercy, and a knowledge . . .
Strange that a knowledge of God should be mentioned last.
    Could it be
    That when I am honest with myself
    And compassionate with others,
    A very special knowledge of the nature of God
    Grows in my heart and mind?

    God, I don't seem to want a watertight theology
    That leaves me higher and drier than anyone else.
    I want to walk barefoot in the rain
    And feel the raindrops on my face
    Until I get so wet
    I shiver from wonder.

The people were astounded by his teaching
– Mark 1:22 KJV

In any situation
When the truly Christian word is spoken,
It is always rather astounding.
It leaves us gasping and objecting.
> *It is the deeply probing word,*
> *That nevertheless is not quite practical*
> *And will get us nowhere . . .*
> *At least not where we were going.*
Yet there it is,
That astounding word that awakens some deep longing
In our hearts,
And makes us wonder if we dare,
In a world of hard realities,
To live by it.

Then Peter spoke:" . . . if you wish it, I will make three shelters
here, one for you, one for Moses, and one for Elijah." . . .
A voice called from the cloud: "Listen . . ."
– Matthew 17:4, 5 NEB

When I see a beautiful thing,
An act of God,
    Whether it be a snowfall,
    A flame,
    A flower,
    Or a human life,
I often say,
This is good!
    I must do something about it,
    I must capture it,
    Recreate it,
    Interpret it,
    Keep it in this form forever!

      But in my hands the flower fades,
      The snowflake melts,
      The flame goes out,
      And the human life grows up and goes away.
        And I am left listening to the voice of God
        The originator and the source
120   *Of beauty.*

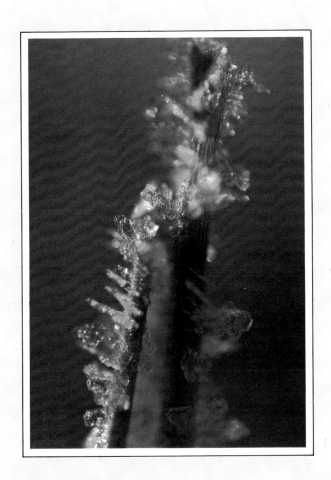

God is our shelter, our strength . . .
so we shall not be afraid when the earth gives
way, when mountains tumble into the depths of the sea . . .
– *Psalm 46:1, 2 TJB*

The gift of life!
One moment on top of the mountain,
The wind on my face
And the horizon endless,
>*The next at the bottom of the sea*
>*Gasping for breath.*

>*God?*
>*What do You have to do with this?*
>*Did You simply give me this life,*
>*And then desert me to make the best of it?*

>*God . . .*
>*Somehow simply knowing You're there,*
>*You're here,*
>*Makes a difference.*
>>*It makes me take the highs easy,*
>>*Knowing they are not forever,*
>>*Because only You are forever.*
>>>*Even the lows can never touch absolute bottom,*
>>>*For You are there,*
>>>*Pushing me up for air,*
>>>*Giving me back my gift of life*
>>>*Again and again. . .and again.*

Subject Index

Scripture Index

DESIGN AND PHOTOGRAPHS BY DAVID KOECHEL

PHOTOS: Pages 19, 75, 76, 97 Dale Beers; Page 65 Paul Bonseigneur;
Page 17 Doug Coleman; Pages 80, 122 John Koeshall;
Page 37 Joe Saussen; Page 3 Larry Swenson.